The Boys' Guide

-

Including Hints on Batting, Bowling, Fielding, and Equipment

British Library Cataloguing-in-Publication Data
A catalogue record for this book is available from the
British Library

A Short History of Cricket

Cricket is a bat-and-ball game played between two teams of eleven players each, on a field at the centre of which is a rectangular twenty-two-yard long pitch. Each team takes its turn to bat, attempting to score runs, while the other team fields. Each turn is known as an innings. Whilst this may sound reasonably simple – the game of cricket has a very long and varied history; changing with time and geographical location.

Early cricket was at some time or other described as 'a club striking a ball (like) the ancient games of club-ball, stool-ball, trap-ball or stob-ball.' The sport can definitely be traced back to Tudor times in early sixteenth century England though. Further written evidence exists of a game known as 'creag' being played by Prince Edward, the son of Edward I, at Newenden, Kent, in 1301. There has been speculation, but no distinct evidence that this was a form of early English cricket.

The earliest definite reference to cricket being played in England (and hence anywhere) is given at a 1598 court case which mentions that 'creckett' was played on common land in Guildford, Surrey around 1550. Here, the court coroner gave witness that 'hee and diverse of his fellows did runne and play [on the common land] at creckett and other plaies.' It is believed that it was originally a children's game but references around 1610 indicate that adults had started playing it and the earliest reference to inter-parish or **village cricket** occurs soon afterwards.   In 1624, a player called **Jasper Vinall** was killed when he was struck on the head during a match between two parish teams in Sussex.

During the seventeenth century, numerous references indicate the growth of cricket in the south-east of England. By the end of the century it had become an organised activity being played for high stakes, and it is believed that the first professionals appeared in the years following the Restoration in 1660. The game underwent major development in the eighteenth century and became the national sport of England. Betting played a major part in that development with rich patrons forming their own 'select XIs'. Bowling only really evolved in 1760 though, when bowlers began to pitch the ball instead of rolling or skimming it towards the batsman. This caused a revolution in bat design because to deal with the bouncing ball, it was necessary to introduce the modern straight bat in place of the old 'hockey stick' shape.   The nineteenth century saw **underarm bowling** replaced by first **roundarm** and then **overarm bowling**. Both developments were controversial.

Meanwhile, the British Empire had been instrumental in spreading the game overseas, and by the middle of the nineteenth century it had become well established in India, North America, the Caribbean, South Africa, Australia and New Zealand. In 1844, the **first international cricket match** took place between the **United States** and **Canada** (although neither has ever been ranked as a Test-playing nation. In 1862, an English team made the first tour of Australia and in 1876–77, an England team took part in the first-ever **Test match** at the **Melbourne Cricket Ground** against **Australia**. The resultant rivalry gave birth to 'The Ashes' in 1882, and this has remained Test cricket's most famous contest ever since.

The last two decades before the First World War have been called the 'Golden Age of Cricket' – a form of nostalgia in the face of mounting modernisation and destruction. It was (and is) a unique game where in addition to the laws of play, the sportsmen must abide by the 'Spirit of the Game.' The standard of sportsmanship has historically been considered so high that the phrase 'it's just not cricket' was coined in the nineteenth century to describe unfair or underhanded behaviour in any walk of life. In the last few decades though, cricket has become increasingly fast-paced and competitive, increasing the use of appealing and **sledging**, although players are still expected to abide by the umpires' rulings without argument, and for the most part they do.

Cricket entered a new era in 1963 when English counties introduced the **limited overs** variant. As it was sure to produce a result, limited overs cricket was lucrative and the number of matches increased. In the twenty-first century, a new limited overs form, **Twenty20,** has made an immediate impact; though its longevity is yet to be established. As is evident from this brief history of Cricket, it is a sport with a long and fascinating history which has firmly retained its popularity into the present day. We hope the reader is encouraged to find out more and maybe have a game of their own.

CRICKET.

BATS.

THE bat is by far the most important item of a cricketer's outfit. His success as a batsman is bound up in no small degree with the good quality of his bat, and its suitability as regards both weight and size.

Weight and Size.—It is a great mistake to use too large, which generally means also too heavy, a bat. Such a bat puts undue strain on the wrists, tires the arm, and prevents the user getting on to a ball quickly.

Quality of Bat.—Great stiffness in the *handle* makes a bat jar the hands and arms. Excessive whippiness is the sign of a weak handle. A good handle should permit a slight amount of bending.

The *blade.*—It is impossible to judge its durability from mere appearance. The striking face should be free of knots, especially in the part which does most of the hitting. As a general rule a red bat is harder than a white one. A straight grain is best.

A boy may well leave the selection of a bat to an expert. If you mean to put a leather or rubber cover on the handle this should be allowed for, so that you may not find yourself with a handle so large that you cannot grip it comfortably.

Care of Bat.—If the blade begins to break up, have it attended to at once. *Pegging* the face is inadvisable, as it often does more harm than good; anyway, amateur pegging is useless. *Wrapping* with waxed string is the best possible protection against splitting and flaking, but should be performed by an expert. Wrapping with surgical adhesive plaster, which becomes extremely sticky when heated, is a simple operation; and if the plaster be put on tightly gives good protection. *Oiling.*—The bat should be rubbed over sparingly with *raw* linseed oil once or twice a week during the season, and once a month when laid by. Keep a bat in a cover of thick

FIG. 17.—England v. Australia at Lord's : Hill and Gregory batting.

[Photo: Sport and General.

CRICKET.

brown paper, so that it may not stain the other things placed in the bag with it.

Cut your initials on the back of the blade near the splice ; and *write* your name and address in indelible ink.

A " sprung " bat, which clicks when struck with, is dangerous to use in a game or match, as likely to cause you to be given out as caught at the wicket.

PADS.

It is essential that these should fit you well enough to allow you to run easily. Pads of the ordinary type, with buckles at the heel and above and below the knee, are preferable to those with a single long strap. The " skeleton " pad is the coolest, and gives excellent protection.

BATTING GLOVES.

Those of the " shield " pattern, studded with rubber spikes, are to be recommended.

Note.—Pads and gloves should *always* be worn in practice and games. A boy who has been hurt once or twice through not wearing them will be inclined to " funk " a dangerous-looking ball.

BOOTS.

Spiked boots should be worn in all matches. It is difficult for a bowler or fielder to do himself justice in smooth-soled boots or shoes. A bowler requires somewhat longer spikes than a fielder.

BALL.

It is advisable that small boys should use an undersized ball, which they can get a proper grip of, handle easily, and throw and hit a good distance. The weight of the ball, as well as of the bat, should be proportioned to the strength and size of the players.

HINTS ON BATTING.

" I am firmly convinced that there is more learnt of the game of cricket by the player being able to see practical illustrations than by studying all the books ever written." Thus that famous cricketer, Mr. W. L. Murdoch, in his book on the game ; and any person of experience will admit the full truth of this. A few minutes of good coaching are worth more than many hours of poring over printed instructions.

Nevertheless, it is safe to assume that a large number of keen youngsters have not the advantage of such coaching, and for their benefit especially the following hints have been put together.

Holding the Bat.—Have the right hand above the middle of the handle. This brings your left hand close to the end, where it should be. It is a mistake to slip the right hand down close to the blade; it cramps your action, diminishes your hitting power, and increases the danger of playing over a ball.

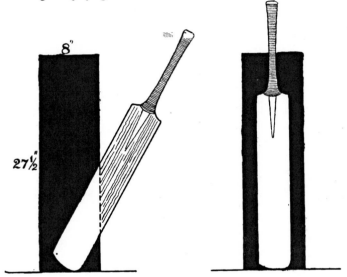

8"

27½"

FIG. 18.—Showing how the wicket (the black rectangle) is protected more fully by a straight than by a sloping bat.

The right hand should grip tightly and not shift. The left naturally moves round from the front to the back as you play forward; and most players find it necessary that it should if the bat is kept upright during the stroke. For driving, cutting, and hitting to leg the left hand remains in front.

How to Stand.—1. When you take up your position at the wicket ask to be given "middle and leg"—that is, such a guard that when your bat is held upright and flat to umpire it shall cover the middle and leg stumps. This is, on the whole, a better guard than "middle," as most boys seem to find it more difficult to protect the leg than the off stump. Another point in its favour is that it renders

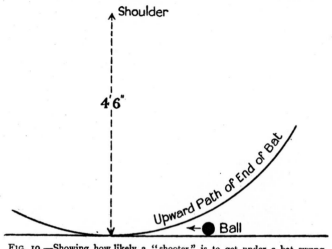

FIG. 19.—Showing how likely a "shooter" is to get under a bat swung in a vertical plane during a "swipe."

you less likely to get leg-before-wicket. Anyway, your toes must be clear of the stumps.

2. Have the right foot behind the popping crease.

3. Put more weight on the right leg than on the left, and keep it still, moving the left leg in the direction of the ball.

4. Stand fairly upright, and don't bend the knees in.

5. Hold your head facing the bowler so that you can see him easily with *both* eyes. Don't watch him round the corner, as it were.

FIG. 20.—Showing the danger of playing across a straight ball. Unless the bat happens to strike the ball while passing from A to B the wicket is lost.

6. Don't fidget. Keep as still as you can.

THE BOYS' GUIDE.

Playing the Ball.—1. Watch the bowler's hand as it comes over, and *keep your eye on the ball*. The importance of doing this cannot be over emphasized.

2. To a well pitched up ball on the wicket, and to all fast balls except very short-pitched ones, play *forward*.

3. In *playing forward* it is essential : (*a*) To hold the bat straight (that is, vertically as seen from in front), so that it may afford the maximum of protection to the stumps (Fig. 18). The left shoulder must be kept well round towards the front and the left elbow out.

(*b*) To bring the left foot forward *simultaneously with*, not before, the bat, and so time the stroke that the bat shall *meet* the ball, not wait for it. This adds greatly to the force of a stroke and minimizes the danger of spooning up a catch.

(*c*) To carry the left foot in the direction of the stroke : straight forward for a straight ball ; slightly to off for a ball on or just outside the off-stump.

(*d*) Not to drag the right foot over the crease and give the wicket-keeper a chance if you miss the ball.

(*e*) To keep the bat low, so that you may stop a low ball and be able to dab down on a "shooter."

(*f*) To look out for variations in pace, and time your stroke accordingly. Don't get stuck by a ball slower than usual.

4. *Don't run out* to fast balls, or any kind of ball on the wicket or on your legs except slow balls (notably underhand "lobs"). Keep your bat straight, and have the handle well forward so that the ball may travel along the ground.

5. Play *back* to short-pitched straight balls, and to very slow balls which you decide not to run out to. On a soft wicket from which the ball gets up slowly back play is advisable. In *playing back :* (*a*) Keep the bat straight.

(*b*) Throw the weight on to the right leg.

(*c*) Let the bat meet the ball, not wait for it.

(*d*) Watch the ball very carefully, as it has more room in which to change its direction and its pace.

6. *Leg Hitting.*—To take a well pitched up ball, put the left leg well forward and hit round to leg. A fast, short ball, coming straight at the legs, should be played out to, not hit. The *glide*, effected by holding the bat at an angle to the ball, so that the latter may glance off it, is now much used ; but the beginner will do well to *leave it alone.*

7. *Cutting.*—(*a*) Don't cut at lobs or slow balls, as there is a great danger of getting underneath them.

CRICKET.

(*b*) Come *down* on the ball, to keep it out of the hands of point and slips. This doesn't mean that a ball should be beaten down so hard as to lose its pace.

(*c*) If a ball is too high to allow you to come down on it, leave it alone.

GENERAL HINTS ON BATTING.

1. Take your guard carefully.

2. Make sure where the fieldsmen are before you face the bowler. You need not do this ostentatiously.

3. Don't dance about while waiting for the ball.

4. Don't bend the right knee as you hit. To do so robs the stroke of half its force.

5. Remember that *placing* the ball is as important as hitting it, if you want to score.

6. Leave alone high and wide balls on the off, and balls that break away from you.

7. Play carefully at first; don't be in too much of a hurry to break your duck's egg.

8. Play *carefully* on a fast wicket, picking out the proper balls for punishment. Long scores require patience and self-control.

9. Don't despise lobs. Very few batsmen can score off them.

10. Regain your wind after running. You can't play correctly while panting and puffing.

11. Don't hit often with all your force. Conserve your energy. Good timing and the use of weight and balance will make a ball travel to the boundary without great exertion on the batsman's part.

12. A hard wicket slightly moistened by rain is still a fast wicket, and equally suited for forward play. It handicaps the bowler more than the batsman.

13. On a sticky wicket it pays to play a forcing (free-hitting) game, as one cannot score on such a wicket by back play.

14. *Keep your right foot still.* Though advanced players move the foot when playing back and cutting, the beginner should not do so. Be very careful in playing a straight full pitch.

15. **Practising at the Nets.**—Don't practise too long or too much. It will only make you stale.

Don't make bad strokes deliberately just because it doesn't matter if you are bowled.

Try to correct known faults, and to cultivate new strokes. A

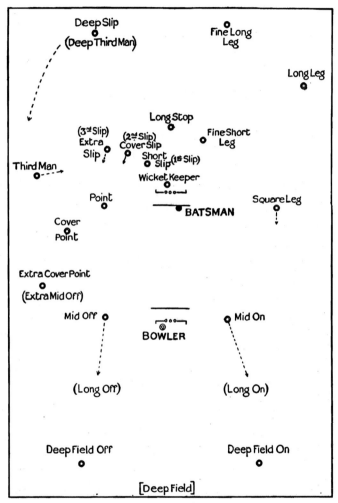

FIG. 21.—Names of stations in the field. Alternative names given in brackets. Arrows denote that the fielder may be moved in the direction indicated.

CRICKET.

one-stroke batsman is rendered comparatively harmless by a judicious arrangement of the fielders.

Don't let the bowlers hustle you. Take your time between strokes.

Five minutes with a bowler who can send the ball where you want it is worth more than half an hour's hitting at erratic deliveries.

Don't imitate other batsmen's styles, but try to improve that which comes to you most naturally.

16. **Running.**—(*a*) The striker should call "Yes" or "No" if the ball goes in front; the non-striker if the ball goes behind. One or the other must call for every ball.

(*b*) If called for a run, and you think you can't manage it, say so quickly and decidedly.

Fig. 22.—Back up; and ground your bat when making a sharp run.

(*c*) Run the first run hard and straight, but well off the wicket, and be ready to run again. Many runs are lost by batsmen over-running and wasting ground.

(*d*) When making a sharp run ground your bat a couple of yards from the home crease and push it along the ground in front of you (Fig. 22).

(*e*) When you are not batting, *back up* well after every delivery (Fig. 22).

(*f*) When you are batting, walk out a few paces after a hit, even if the ball is going to a near fielder. If he "muffs" the ball, part of your run will have been made and you will have a good chance of completing it.

FIG. 23.—Signals used in umpiring.

CRICKET.

(*g*) Backing up must not be interpreted as a call to run.

(*h*) Make allowances for a batsman who is a slower runner than yourself.

(*i*) Look out for the overthrows.

BOWLING.

There are probably more "naturally" good batsmen than bowlers; but it is impossible to say how much the really good bowler owes to inborn capacity and how much to perseverance and the close study of the principles of bowling. Every first-class bowler has practised diligently to attain his proficiency. On the other hand, many prom-

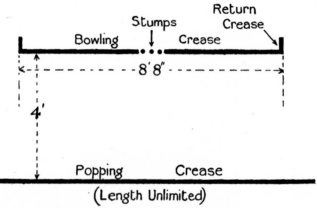

FIG. 24.—Dimensions and spacing of creases.

ising bowlers have failed because they shirked the drudgery of constant practice.

So, though you have not made your mark as a bowler, and may even have a reputation for sending down "soft stuff," don't assume that you can never hope to make your deliveries respected.

Begin by ridding yourself of the idea that high speed and a sensational "break" are the great things to aim at. Far more important than either of these are *straightness* and *good length*. When you have acquired these, you may begin to think of increasing your pace and putting "work" on the ball.

THE BOYS' GUIDE.

HINTS ON BOWLING.

1. Young boys should use a ball small enough for them to get their hands round, and light enough not to tire their arms unduly. For boys under fourteen a 21-yard or even shorter pitch is preferable to the 22-yard. The extra few yards make an immense deal of difference in the amount of effort required from the bowler.

2. To acquire *straightness* of delivery, practise at a single stump; then at one stump out of three; and finally cultivate the art of sending a ball just outside the off-stump.

3. "Bowl at the off-stump" is a good rule.

4. To acquire a *good length*, which, more than anything else, puzzles a batsman, practise pitching the ball on to a disc of paper. Shift the disc occasionally.

Note.—Good length varies with pace. For a slow ball it may be 3 to 4 yards, for a fast ball 5 to 7 yards, from the crease.

5. Find out what amount of run to the wicket suits you best, and stick to it. Don't run 5 yards for one ball, and 10 yards for another. A long run doesn't necessarily increase the pace.

6. Don't hesitate before delivering the ball. Run and delivery should be all in one piece, as it were.

7. Keep the hand and head well up. A descending ball is harder to watch than one travelling more horizontally.

8. Turn your body edgeways to the batsman as you deliver the ball. This makes it more difficult for him to watch the ball as it leaves the hand.

9. *Vary your pace*, but not too often, or the batsman will be on the lookout; not too much, or he won't be deceived. It requires a lot of practice to deliver fast and slow balls with the same action. Ability to do so makes great bowlers.

10. Vary the length when you vary the pace; the faster the ball, the farther from the crease should it pitch.

11. Don't bowl as fast as you can; don't increase your pace after you have been hit; and don't continue bowling when you feel tired. Take or ask for a rest.

12. Don't hurry yourself. Take plenty of time between every two balls.

13. Grip the ball with the fingers, not with the palm, if you wish to make it "break."

14. Try to find out the batsman's weak spot.

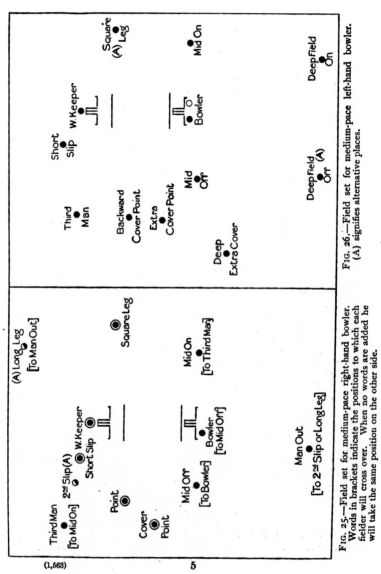

FIG. 25.—Field set for medium-pace right-hand bowler. Words in brackets indicate the positions to which each fielder will cross over. When no words are added he will take the same position on the other side.

FIG. 26.—Field set for medium-pace left-hand bowler. (A) signifies alternative places.

15. A bad batsman often succumbs to a rather short ball just outside the off-stump. He gets under it and sends it to slip.

16. Until you have mastered a break from one side don't try to make the ball break from the other. In many cases a bowler spoils his most natural break by cultivating the alternative.

17. An occasional "yorker" is dangerous to the batsman.

18. Practise bowling round as well as over the wicket. A change of side tends to upset a batsman.

19. Learn to put down the wicket when the ball is returned from the field during a run.

20. Keep cool; and don't get angry and try to bowl faster if your bowling is punished.

21. Remember that you have ten colleagues to assist you in getting the batsman out, and that the positions of several of them should be arranged to suit *your* bowling. Try to find out what arrangement is most effective.

HINTS ON FIELDING.

Some cricketers get their place in the team simply on account of their good fielding. A run saved is as good as a run gained.

1. Don't stand with your feet wide apart, as you have to bring them together before you can move.

2. Put your heels together when fielding a straight ground ball.

3. Return the ball to the bowler or wicket-keeper either as a long hop or an easy catch. The bowler should not have to stoop to gather the ball; it tires him.

4. Send the ball back promptly but not wildly.

5. Always "back up" a throw in. Keep well away from the man you are backing up, so that you may have time to watch the ball if it passes him.

6. A high catch should be taken with the finger tips about level with the chin.

7. Don't go wool-gathering when things are quiet, lest when your chance does come you may not be ready to take it.

8. Stand on your toes more than on your heels.

BOOKS ON CRICKET.

"**Cricket for Beginners.**" By A. C. Maclaren. (George Routledge and Sons. 1s.) The best book for the boy who wishes to improve

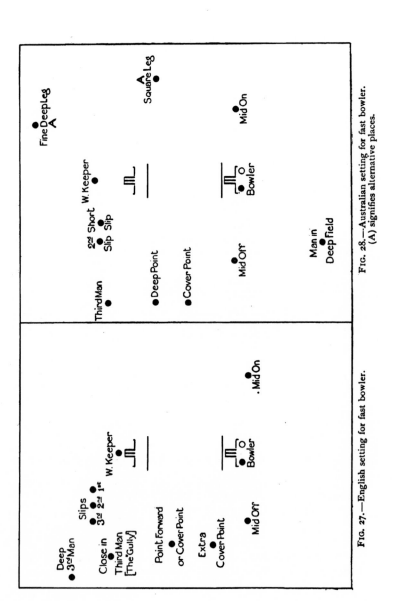

FIG. 27.—English setting for fast bowler.

FIG. 28.—Australian setting for fast bowler. (A) signifies alternative places.

THE BOYS' GUIDE.

his cricket all round. The letterpress is pithy, and valuable through-
out as coming from the pen of one of our leading batsmen. The
twenty-three photographic illustrations show how strokes should and
should not be made. A series of diagrams explain how to place the
fieldsmen to suit different classes of bowling and different conditions
of the pitch. There is a very useful chapter on *captaincy*, of which
Mr. Maclaren has had wide experience, both as a boy and a man.

"**Cricket.**" By W. L. Murdoch. (George Routledge and Sons.
1s.) Mr. Murdoch, the old Australian captain, treats his subject very
thoroughly in this book. Of the eighty-six pages, thirty are devoted
to batting, twenty to fielding, and fifteen to bowling. Strongly
advised.

"**The Complete Cricketer.**" By A. E. Knight. (Methuen and
Co. 10s. 6d. net.) Includes, besides the usual subjects, chapters on
the history of the game, past and present players, cricket in Australia,
and modern cricket and its problems. It contains an excellent
glossary of cricket terms. Very interesting.

"**Cricket.**" (Badminton Library Series.) By A. G Steel, the Hon.
R. H. Lyttleton, A. Lang, W. G. Grace, and R. A. H. Mitchell.
(Longmans, Green, and Co.) The most valuable chapter of this
excellent work is, so far as boys are concerned, that on "The Art of
Training Young Cricketers," by Mr. R. A. H. Mitchell.

"**Great Batsmen, Their Methods at a Glance.**" By George W.
Beldam and Charles B. Fry. (Macmillan and Co., Ltd.) Contains
over 600 reproductions of instantaneous photographs, many of them
really very wonderful examples of what can be done with the camera.
Batsmen shown in all stages of making various strokes. Valuable
explanatory notes by Mr. Fry.

"**Great Bowlers and Fielders.**" By the same authors. (Macmillan
and Co., Ltd.) A companion volume to "Great Batsmen." These
books are even more valuable than the actual watching of players, as
eye impressions are fleeting, whereas the camera's record is fixed and
permanent.

[I have to thank Mr. E. H. Parry for his kind revision of this
chapter, and Capt. E. G. Wynyard for assistance given in connection
with the diagrams showing positions of fielders.]

Lightning Source UK Ltd.
Milton Keynes UK
UKOW04f1351110315

247690UK00001B/86/P